**Ramesh Sekaran**
**Abirami Ragupathi**

**Feature Based Opinion Summarization using Transfer Learning**

Ramesh Sekaran
Abirami Ragupathi

# Feature Based Opinion Summarization using Transfer Learning

## Research Perspective

LAP LAMBERT Academic Publishing

**Impressum / Imprint**

Bibliografische Information der Deutschen Nationalbibliothek: Die Deutsche Nationalbibliothek verzeichnet diese Publikation in der Deutschen Nationalbibliografie; detaillierte bibliografische Daten sind im Internet über http://dnb.d-nb.de abrufbar.

Alle in diesem Buch genannten Marken und Produktnamen unterliegen warenzeichen-, marken- oder patentrechtlichem Schutz bzw. sind Warenzeichen oder eingetragene Warenzeichen der jeweiligen Inhaber. Die Wiedergabe von Marken, Produktnamen, Gebrauchsnamen, Handelsnamen, Warenbezeichnungen u.s.w. in diesem Werk berechtigt auch ohne besondere Kennzeichnung nicht zu der Annahme, dass solche Namen im Sinne der Warenzeichen- und Markenschutzgesetzgebung als frei zu betrachten wären und daher von jedermann benutzt werden dürften.

Bibliographic information published by the Deutsche Nationalbibliothek: The Deutsche Nationalbibliothek lists this publication in the Deutsche Nationalbibliografie; detailed bibliographic data are available in the Internet at http://dnb.d-nb.de.

Any brand names and product names mentioned in this book are subject to trademark, brand or patent protection and are trademarks or registered trademarks of their respective holders. The use of brand names, product names, common names, trade names, product descriptions etc. even without a particular marking in this work is in no way to be construed to mean that such names may be regarded as unrestricted in respect of trademark and brand protection legislation and could thus be used by anyone.

Coverbild / Cover image: www.ingimage.com

Verlag / Publisher:
LAP LAMBERT Academic Publishing
ist ein Imprint der / is a trademark of
OmniScriptum GmbH & Co. KG
Heinrich-Böcking-Str. 6-8, 66121 Saarbrücken, Deutschland / Germany
Email: info@lap-publishing.com

Herstellung: siehe letzte Seite /
Printed at: see last page
**ISBN: 978-3-659-71794-9**

# ACKNOWLEDGEMENT

Writing a monograph is a drop from continuous journey in research. The journey of research is not alone; it is journey of thousand miles taking many challenges and many great minds together. It is a pleasure to thank those who made this monograph possible such as my Father who gave me the moral support I required and my Project associate Ms. R. ABIRAMI who helped me with the research material. I am thankful to LAP LAMBERT Academic Publisher and I would like to acknowledge the editing team led by Tatiana Melnic. I am very thankful to the Dean and Head of CSE, Anna University Regional Office, Madurai for giving me the great opportunity for writing this monograph.

**Dr. S. RAMESH**

# DEDICATION

*To my Parents*

# TABLE OF CONTENTS

# LIST OF FIGURES

# LIST OF TABLES

# CHAPTER I

# INTRODUCTION

## 1.1 OVERVIEW

The vast majority of the existing method use single domain corpus to perform the feature based opinion mining. Different domain needs different method to perform feature extraction and opinion prediction. The feature and opinion words are identified through Part-of-Speech (PoS) tagging methodology. POS tagging is process of identify the part-of-speech of given input sentence. Based on this POS outcome we have to identify the features and opinion word. Normally feature in the form of noun and opinion word in the form of adjective and verb.

Inter Dependent Domain Relevance performs the feature extraction in two different domains to reduce the complexity of feature extraction in different domain. The feature extraction and pruning is the first steps of the feature based opinion mining using inter dependent domain relevance. These approaches extract the features of two different domains at the same time. The extraction is depends on domain relevance score and threshold value.

The opinion prediction is done with the help of Exaggerate Instance weighted K nearest neighbor (EIWKNN). It classifies each opinion words using the source labeled data. Cross validation is first step of the EIWKNN algorithm. It improves the accuracy of the classifier. The accuracy of the classifier can be increased during each round of the cross validation until it reach the maximum accuracy. The class of the unlabeled word can be predicted based on the nearest neighbor class and weight value. The K number of nearest neighbor is identified through the Hamming Distance.

Normally the opinion classification only considers the opinion word. Sometimes the polarity (Opinion) of the opinion word can change due to the prior polarity word. EIWKNN approach considers the prior polarity before it finalizes the polarity of the opinion word. The summarization is the final step of the feature based opinion summarization. The summarization is in the form of each feature with their corresponding strongly positive, weakly positive, strongly negative, weakly negative and neutral opinion sentence.

## 1.2 OBJECTIVE

To improve the decision makingof new user in various domains such as product, movie, news media, social networking shares etc. we are going to the Feature based opinion summarization. The feature based opinion summarization classifies the given user reviews into strongly positive, weakly positive, strongly negative, weakly negative and then summarize the sentence with their corresponding feature. The features and opinion words are identifies by Part-Of-Speech tagging. The main objective is performing the two different domain feature based opinion summarization using Transfer learning. Initially the features are extracted from two different domain using inter dependent domain relevance (IDDR) score and Opinion is classified using Exaggerate Instance weighted K nearest neighbor (EIWKNN). The Exaggerate Instance weighted K nearest neighbor (EIWKNN) algorithm is to transfer the knowledge from camera domain to iPod domain.

2

## 1.3 SCOPE OF THE MONOGRAPH

The purpose of the monograph is to summarize the customer reviews in the form of each features and corresponding strongly positive, weakly positive, neutral, strongly negative, weakly negative. First step is to extract the common features and most important features present in the Canon S100 and iPod reviews. Second step is to classify the user reviews. Finally summarize the feature with their corresponding opinion sentences.

The scope of project is to summarize the two different domain reviews concurrently with high efficient manner via feature extraction, transfer learning and classification algorithm. The Inter Dependent Domain Relevance (IDDR) mechanism is extracting the relevant and contrast domain features using domain relevance score. Exaggerate Instance Weighted K-Nearest Neighbor algorithm is perform classification through knowledge transfer.

## 1.4 OPINION MINING

Large volume of online information such as documents, files, web pages, books, news media present in the web. Due to this information web mining carries in three different kinds of process such as web content mining, web usage mining and web structure mining. Web content mining is the process of extracting knowledge from web page content; Web usage mining is the extraction of the models and patterns store the activities of the user and gather the user requirements; Web structure mining is way to discover the knowledge of hyperlinks to maximize the relation between the web pages (Bing Liu et al,2011). The opinion mining is from the web content mining and it performs the prediction of sentiment of the new document or sentence or review through the gathering of emotions, sentiments, thoughts from the previous reviews, documents and sentences.

Basically opinion mining has several types they are Document based opinion mining, Sentence based opinion mining and Feature based opinion mining. Document based opinion mining is simple classify the document as positive, negative, neutral etc. Sentence level opinion mining has two different tasks such as Subjective classification and opinion Classification. Subjective classification is to classify the sentence into subjective or objective. Consider the example 'I went the movie yesterday' is objective, 'The movie is nice' is subjective. Opinion classification is to classify the opinion as positive, negative, neutral etc. The feature based opinion mining identifies the features and predict the positive, negative, neutral opinion are belonging to that features.

## 1.5 TRANSFER LEARNING

A major assumption in data mining and machine learning approach is that the training and test data must be in the same domain shown in figure 1.1. In many real world applications, the above assumption is not possible. The gathering of labeled data in every domain is not possible in every data mining process. In such cases move to the transfer learning to perform operation more effectively through avoiding much expensive data. Transfer learning shown in Figure 1.2.has proven to be promising in real-world applications, e.g., text categorization, sentiment analysis, image classification, video summarization, and collaborative filtering, etc.

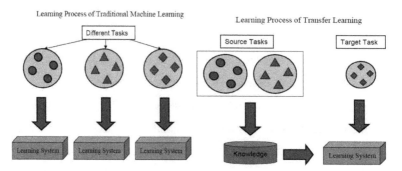

Figure 1.1. Traditional Machine Learning          Figure 1.2. Transfer Learning

One major computational problem of transfer learning is how to explore the shared knowledge structure underlying input domains as the bridge to propagate supervision information from the source domains to the target domains. The main limitation of most prior transfer learning methods is that they do not simultaneously preserve both the statistical property and geometric structure.

In reality, preserving these complementary properties together is important to make learning models robust to the domain difference. In some difficult scenarios, the intrinsic domain structure cannot be effectively explored with a single property of data. In this case, previous methods may suffer from ineffective transfer, i.e., underfitting the target data. In other difficult scenarios, the domain difference can be so large that it may be difficult to extract common factors as the bridge for knowledge transfer. In this case, previous methods may suffer from negative transfer, i.e., overfitting the target data.

For the ineffective transfer problem, inspired by Zhu et al., the statistical and geometric properties may focus on different aspects of the original data and are complementary to each other in reality. The justifications are as follows. On one hand, each data point may be associated with some latent factors. For example, a text document can be regarded as a combination of several hidden semantics. Extracting these latent factors involves preserving the statistical property of the original data (Ding C. et al,2006).

On the other hand, from the geometric perspective, the data points may be sampled from a distribution supported by a low-dimensional manifold embedded in a high-dimensional space (Cai D.et al,2011) Preserving this geometric structure involves encoding similar examples or features with similar embedding. By preserving the statistical and geometric properties together, to improve the smoothness of latent factors and enhance the effectiveness of transfer learning.

## 1.6 LAZY LEARNING

Lazy learning is a learning method in which the system performs operation after the query is sent to the classifier as opposed to in eager learning where the system tries to performs the operation before it receives queries. For lazy learning, the training set is the most important part because such lazy behavior completely depends on the abundant memory as a strong supporter. Unfortunately, in some cases, this knowledge memory is not that strong and even poor to support lazy learning due to the lack of information such as inadequate training data and new queries.

Especially, traditional lazy learning method work well when the training and test data are drawn from a same data source and training and testing data are drawn from a same data source and feature space. Once there comes a new query and the training memory is accumulated from similar but different data source, learning model has to be rebuilt, which is expensive or even impossible.

## 1.7 NEAREST NEIGHBOR

K Nearest Neighbor (KNN) is one of those algorithms that are very simple to understand but works incredibly well in practice. Also it is surprisingly versatile and its applications range from vision to proteins to computational geometry to graphs and so on. Most people learn the algorithm and do not use it much which is a pity as a clever use of KNN can make things very simple.

It is also a lazy algorithm. What this means is that it does not use the training data points to do any generalization. In other words, there is no explicit training phase or it is very minimal. This means the training phase is pretty fast. Lack of generalization means that KNN keeps all the training data. More exactly, all the training data is needed during the testing phase. (Well this is an exaggeration, but not far from truth). This is in contrast to other techniques like Support Vector Machine where you can discard all non-support vectors without any problem. Most of the lazy algorithms – especially KNN – make decision based on the entire training data set (in the best case a subset of them).

KNN assumes that the data is in a feature space. More exactly, the data points are in a metric space. The data can be scalars or possibly even multidimensional vectors. Since the points are in feature space, they have a notion of distance – This need not necessarily be Euclidean distance although it is the one commonly used.

Each of the training data consists of a set of vectors and class label associated with each vector. In the simplest case, it will be either + or − (for positive or negative classes). KNN can work equally well with arbitrary number of classes. We are also given a single number "k". This number decides how many neighbors (where neighbors are defined based on the distance metric) influence the classification. This is usually an odd number if the number of classes is 2. If k=1, then the algorithm is simply called the nearest neighbor algorithm.

The Exaggerate Instance Weighted K-Nearest Neighbor algorithm performs the classification with great accurate classifier. Cross validation is the process to improve and identify the accuracy of the classifier. The accuracy of the classifier can be increased during each round of the cross validation until it reach the maximum accuracy.

Normally the opinion classification only considers the opinion word. Sometimes the polarity (Opinion) of the opinion word can change due to the prior polarity word. EIWKNN approach consider the prior polarity before it finalize the polarity of the opinion word

## 1.8 THE PART-OF-SPEECH TAGGING

The Part-Of-Speech tagging is the method of extracting the Part-Of-Speech of each word given in the input space. The features and opinions are extracted with help of the Part-Of-Speech tagging tools. Several free tools available in online or offline to extract the features and opinion from the given reviews. Opinion words are adjectives and features are nouns.

Consider the following example. "This is good book" – this/DT is/VBZ good/JJ book/NN.

In above sentence, book (product feature) is noun (NN) and good (opinion word) is adjective (JJ). In Part-Of-Speech tagging, each word in review is tagged with its Part-Of-Speech such as noun(NN), adverb (RB), verb(VB), conjunction (CC),pronoun (PRP) etc.

After POS tagging, now it is ready to retrieve nouns as features and adjectives as opinion words. There are differently freely available POS taggers like Stanford POS tagger, Tree tagger, CRF tagger etc. Normally opinion mining use single domain to classify their thoughts. Some researcher's perform cross domain sentiment classification to improve the performance of the classification.

## 1.9 DISTANCE MEASURES

In information theory, the Hamming distance between two strings of equal length is the number of positions at which the corresponding symbols are different. In another way, it measures the minimum number of substitutions required to change one string into the other, or the minimum number of errors that could have transformed one string into the other.

The Hamming distance between:

- "karolin" and "kathrin" is 3.
- "karolin" and "kerstin" is 3.
- 1011101 and 1001001 is 2.
- 2173896 and 2233796 is 3.

## 1.10 DOMAIN RELEVANCE SCORE

Domain relevance score is calculates with the help of the Dispersion and Deviation. The Dispersion is calculated on basis of average weight and Standard Variance of each term present in the candidate features. Deviation is examined by average weight of each document and weight for term in the candidate features.

Based on domain relevance score, the features present in various reviews can be selected for classification. Initially the features are extracted and pruned. Finally the relevant features only selected for further classification.

## 1.11 ORGANIZATION OF THE MONOGRAPH

The organization of the Monograph is as follows.

The Chapter II shows the Literature Survey, in which the various Opinion Mining Techniques are discussed.

The Chapter III depicts the Feature Extraction mechanism called Inter Dependent Domain Relevance Mechanism are discussed.

The Chapter IV portrays the Overall system architecture and Opinion Classification mechanism called Exaggerate Instance Weighted K-Nearest Neighbor is discussed.

The Chapter V describes about the System Requirements Specification and the Experimental results of EIWKNN algorithm.

The report is wrapped up with the conclusion.

# CHAPTER II

# LITERATURE SURVEY

## 2.1 INTRINSIC AND EXTRINSIC DOMAIN RELEVANCE

Normally features are extracted or patterns are mined from a single review corpus. The features extracted from a multiple review corpus have been conducted in domain specific corpus and domain independent corpus. Domain independent corpus is contrast to the domain specific corpus. The features are extracted from the reviews termed as Candidate features.

The opinion features are identified based on the Domain Relevance (Zhen Hai, Kuiyu Changet al,2014) value. The domain relevance is used to check whether the term is related to the particular review or corpus or not. The domain relevance value is predicted with the help of the dispersion and deviation.The dispersion is identified how frequency a term is used across all documents by measuring the distributional significance of the term across different document in the whole domain. The deviation quantifies how frequently a term is used in a particular document by measuring its distributional significance in the document. The dispersion and deviation are calculated with the help of the frequency-inverse document frequency (TF-IDF) term weight.

IDR/EDR and IEDR algorithms are used to extracted candidate features and pruned the irrelevant features. The Domain relevance score is calculated for examined the Relevance of features for each term in across all documents.

The extract of relevant features using threshold value as follows.

If$(idr_i \geq i^{th})$ AND $(edr_i \leq e^{th})$ then confirm $CF_i$ as feature.

$idr_i$ - domain specific domain relevance score

$edr_i$ - domain independent domain relevance score

$i^{th}, e^{th}$ are threshold value for domain specific and independent corpus.

## 2.2 EXTRACTING PRODUCT FEATURES AND OPINION FROM REVIEWS

A. Popescu and O. Etzioni, (2005) has proposed that the product reviews are crawled and find the opinions related to the product. The rating is available in the website to describe the opinion about the product. Hotel reviews are considered and predict the opinion about the particular hotel.

They split their problem of review mining into the four subtasks. (1) Identify product features; (2) Identify opinions regarding product features ; (3) Determine the polarity of opinions; (4) Rank opinions based on their strength Unsupervised information extracted provides the solution to each of the above subtasks.

OPINE method have two inputs like product reviews and product class. The output is a set contain the features and ranked opinion list.

Steps involved in OPINE method is described below.

(i)    The reviews(R) are parsed with the help of MINIPAR parse. The parser review is assigned as R.

(ii)   Find the explicit (identified form the sentence) feature using parsed review (R') and product class(c). The explicit feature is assigned as 'E'.

(iii)   The opinion about the explicit feature is identified using parsed review (R). The opinion is assigned as 'O'.

(iv)   The opinions are clusters and clusters opinion is CO.

(v)   Using the clustered opinion explicit features and implicit features are gathered.

(vi)   Finally the Rank is produced using Clustered opinion.

(vii)   The final set is produced using Ranked Opinion and Explicit, implicit features. The set contain each feature and associated opinions.

Opinion phrases are extracted the opinioned word may be adjective, verb, noun or adverb phrases. The opinions can be positive or negative and vary strength. The point wise mutual information between the phrases that is estimated from web search engine hit counts.OPINE, a review-mining system whose components include the use of relaxation labeling to find the semantic orientation of words in the given products and sentence. Predict the opinion belonging to each feature.

## 2.3 SENTIWORDNET

Andrea Esuli_ and Fabrizio Sebastiani(2006) has quoted that Opinion about product and political candidates are used in SentiWordNet. The automatic extraction of opinion of PN-polarity of subjective term word net is used to estimate the opinion into three numerical scores. They are obj(s), pos(s), neg(s). Identify how the term contained in SYNSET, 3 scores are derived by combining the results produced by a committee of eight ternary classifier.

Within opinion mining, several subtasks are available; (1) Determining text SO-polarity - Decide whether a given sentence has a factual feature (describes a given situation or event without describing a positive or negative opinion on it) or expresses an opinion in the form of subject. The given text is categories into two forms. One is subject and another one is object. The object is further classified as positive and negative. (2) Determining Text PN polarity - Finding whether the given text expresses positive or a negative opinion on its subject matter. (3) Determining the strength of text PN-polarity - After finding the polarity of the text, check the strength of the polarity like weakly positive, mildly positive, strongly positive, weakly negative, mildly negative, strongly negative.

## 2.4 THUMBS UP OR THUMBS DOWN?

P.D. Turney (2002) has explained a simple unsupervised learning algorithm is used to classify the reviews in the form of recommended (thumbs up) or not recommended (thumbs down). The classification is carried on with the help of semantic orientation of the given phrases in the reviews that contain adjective and adverbs. The association is predicted based on semantic orientation. The good association is revealed by positive semantic orientation, the bad association is revealed by negative sematic orientation. The average sematic orientation is calculated, based on this decision is made. Finally the classification is done as review is recommended or not recommended.

The PMI-IR (Point wise Mutual Information- Information Retrieval) algorithm is to estimate the sematic orientation of a phrase. This method has measure the similarity of pair of words or phrases to a positive reference word("Excellent") with its similarity to a negative reference word("poor").

(i)    Extract phrases containing adjectives or adverbs: Some complexity will arise adjectives, consider an example "unpredictable". It is negative sentiment in automobiles reviews like "unpredictable steering". Other word it is positive sentiment in movie reviews like "unpredictable plot". The algorithm extracts two consecutive words, one is adjective or adverb another one is context provider. Part-of-speech tagger is applied to the review and obtains those two consecutive words. The third pattern conveys that the first two words are adjective and the third word cannot be a noun. Then that sentence is taken as input for algorithm.

(ii)    Estimate the semantic orientation of the extracted phrase using PMI-IR algorithm. The PMI of any tow extracted words (word1 and word2) is defined as follows

PMI(word1,word2)=log2[p(word1 and word2)\p(word1) p(word2)]→ (2.1)

PMI(word1 and word2) means that the problem of co-occurrence of word1 and word2. PMI(word1 and word2) shows the dependency between the two words. The semantic orientation of a phrase is calculated from (A). the reference word like "excellent" and "poor" were be chosen because the rating for poor is one and Excellent is five. The semantic orientation is positive when the phrase is strongly associated with excellent and semantic orientation is negative when the phrase is strongly associated with poor. The number of hits for a given query is hits(query). The co-occurance is interpreted as NEAR.

$$SO(phrase) = log_2 \left[ \frac{hits(phrase\ NEAR\ ``excellent")\ hits(``poor")}{hits(phrase\ NEAR\ ``poor")\ hits(``excellent")} \right] \rightarrow (2.2)$$

To avoid divide by zero exception adding 0.01 to the hits value. To avoid the phrase contain list less than four(i.e. both hits(phrase NEAR "excellent") and hits(phrase NEAR "poor") were simultaneous less then four).

(iii)    Aggregate the SO of the phrase in the given review and predict that reiew is recommended or not recommended. If the value of the semantic orientation is positive, then the review is recommended. If the value of semantic orientation is negative, then the review is not recommended.

The input for the algorithm is reviews and the output is the classification i.e. recommended or not recommended. The PMI-IR(Point wise Mutual Information- Information Retrieval) algorithm is to estimate the sematic orientation of a phrase. This method has measure the similarity of pair of words or phrases to a positive reference word("Excellent") with its similarity to a negative reference word("poor").

## 2.5 STRUCTURE AWARE REVIEW MINING

According to F. Li et.alfrom reference (2010)Feature based review summarization. This approach is different from most of previous work with linguistics rule or statistical method. Joint structure tagging method for review mining using conditional random field mechanism. Rich features to jointly extract the positive, negative opinion and object feature is made. Linguistics representation is integrated into modular representation, instead of linear chain. The design structure and syntactic tree structure is created (object feature in which the opinion expressed on). The generation of summarization is more useful to new users and producers. Basically the opinions are ranked by their frequency.

The basic three steps are

(1) Feature, opinion pair extraction.

(2) Polarity prediction.

(3) Each object relevant opinion extract the object features and positive and negative opinion present in the review.

Use skip-chain CRF's and tree CRFs to utilize conjunction structure and syntactic tree structure. The structure aware denotes the output structure, which models the relationship among the output labels. The linguistic structure refers to the input structure methods or input features for classification. Opinion topic identification is somewhat difficult. There is no prelimit of topics in advance. First they identify an opinion, the opinion holder and topic. The opinion holder is an entity who holds an opinion and topic is what the opinion is deals. Finally the output is like a triples store<opnion, holder, topic> in a database. FrameNet data is used by mapping target words to opinion bearing words and mapping semantic roles to holders, topic and the use them for system training.

Example: "good pictures and beautiful music"
Adjective: "good" and "beautiful" and Noun: "picture" and "music"

If the nearest distance exceeds the threshold, the skip edge will be discarded. Consider one example having the threshold value as '9'.In linear-chain structure and skip chain structure, "like" and "movie" has no direct edge, but in syntactic tree "movie" is directly connected with "like" and their relationship "dobj" is also included which shown "movie" is an objective of "like". The tree CRFs to model the syntactic tree structure for review mining.

Each node is corresponding to a word in the dependency tree. The edge is corresponding to dependency tree edges.

## 2.6 EXTRACTING OPINIONS, OPINION HOLDERS AND TOPIC.

S.-M. Kim and E. Hovy, (2006)has elaborated that the method for identification an opinion with its holder and topic of online news media text. The method of exploiting semantic structure of a sentence attached to an opinion bearing as adjective or verb semantic role labeling method is used as intermediate step to label an opinion holder and topic using data from FrameNet.

Task is decomposed into three phrases.

(1) Identify the opinion word

(2) Labeling semantic roles related to the word in the sentence

(3) Finding the holder and topic of the opinion word among the labeled semantic roles.

Clustering technique is used to predict the frame for a word, which occur most probably and is not defined in FrameNet. Traditionally researches are based on identifying opinion expression and subjective words/phrases. They less concentrate on subjectivity and polarity such as opinion holders, topic of opinion and intertopic/ inter-topic relationships.

The different thought holders are aggregated and find the opinion on social and politicals issues leads to better understanding of the relationship among people or organization or countries. Product review consider product itself or its specific features such as design, quality etc. but the news media different from that. It focuses on social issues, governs acts, news event or some one's opinion. Opinion topic identification is somewhat difficult. There is no prelimit of topics in advance.

First they identify an opinion, the opinion holder and topic. The opinion holder is an entity who holds an opinion and topic is what the opinion is deals. Finally the output is like a triples store<opinion, holder, topic> in a database. FrameNet data is used by mapping target words to opinion bearing words and mapping semantic roles to holders, topic and the use them for system training. It is representing unified model with two dependencies. Skip tree CRFs is to combine two structure namely tree and skip i.e. Joint structure tagging.

## 2.7 RECOGNIZING CONTEXTUAL POLARITY

T. Wilson, J. Wiebe, and P. Hoffmann (2005) has quoted that Phrase level sentiment analysis is carried out. Initially it checks whether an expression is neutral or polar. Automatic identification of contextual polarity for lare subset is done. Sometimes the entries are tagged with priori prior polarity. They create corpus and add contextual polarity judgment to the existing annotations in the multi-perspective question answering (mpqa) opinion corpus annotations of subjective expressions.

Subjective expressions is any word or phrase used to express an opinion, emotion, evaluation, speculation etc. annotators were instructed to tag the polarity of subjective expression as positive, negative, both or neutral. The positive tag for positive emotions (I'm happy), evaluations(great idea!) and stances (she supports the bill). The negative tag is for negative emotions (I'm sad). Evaluation (bad idea!) and stances (she's against the bill). The both tag is for positive and negative. The neutral tag- all othe subjective expression, speculation and those tha do not have positive or negative polarity.

Example 1: thousands of coup supporters celebrated(positive) overnight, waving flags......

Example 2: The three countries in questions are repressive(negative).

Example 3: Besides, politicians refer to good and evil (both) only for purposes of intimidation and exaggeration.

Example 4: Jerome says the hospital feels(neutral) no different than a hospital in the states

The annotators were to judge the contextual polarity of the sentiment. Example the subjective expression. They have not succeeded and will never succeed was marked as positive in the sentence. They have not succeeded and will never succeed, in breaking the will of this valiant people. The reasoning is that breaking the will of a valiant people is negative; hence not succeeding in breaking their will is positive.

## 2.8 MOVIE REVIEW MINING AND SUMMARIZATION

L. Zhuang, Feng Jing and Xiaoyan Zhu (2006) has focused on specific domain called movie review. Multi-knowledge based approach is proposed which include wordnet, statistical analysis and movie knowledge. Mining and summarization method is different from text mining. Initially identification of the feature is carried out, then identifies the opinions wordnet is used to generate a keyword list using movie cast and labeled training data.

The grammatical rules are used to identify the features and opinion pair. Finally organize the sentence. Most of the review mining and summarization is concentrate on product reviews. They focus on different domain called movie review. It has unique characteristics. The user wrote a comment for a particular movie not only a movie element (e.g. screenplay, vision effects, music) and also movie-related people (director, actor and screenwriter).

The tasks are decomposed into several subtasks.

(1) Identify features word and opinion word.

(2) Determine the class of the feature word and polarity of the opinion word.

(3) For each feature word identify the relevant opinion word, and then produce feature-opinion pair.

(4) Finally delivery the summary in the form of features and opinion pair.

Product features are extracted; features are combined with the nearest opinion word.Summary was produced by selecting and re-organizing the sentence according to the extracted features. Expand the opinion word list by adding noun.Subjective classification: the task of subjective classification is to distinguish sentences, paragraphs or documents the present opinions and evaluations from sentences that objectively present factual information. Subjective classification does not need semantic orientation and does not need to find features word an opinion words.Review mining need not only find features, but also determine the semantic orientation of opinions.

## 2.9 LIKELIHOOD RATIO TEST

According to, Zhen Hai, Kuiyu Changet.alfrom reference (2010) normally systematic techniques are applied to the feature based sentiment identification from Chinese reviews. The feature detection is carried out using the syntactic rules after detecting the features; the irrelevant features are pruned using relevance score. Likelihood ratio test is applied to the opinion word to classify the sentence into positive and negative via association rules. The semantic association is measured between the positive word and each seed word by likelihood ratio test. The classification is performed after the association rules by opinion value, upper bound and lower bound.

## 2.10 INSTANCE WEIGHTED K NEAREST NEIGHBOR

P. Sanju et.al (2013) has explained that in Traditional Machine learning, training and test distribution are same for classification. However in many real world applications, this assumption may not hold. The problem of building the classification model for a target class tends to be helpless due to the lack of information such as inadequate labeling data. They use an Adaptive Transfer learning in which the knowledge is learned from the source domain and it is applied to the target domain. They use an adaptive transfer learning for classifying data in power generation dataset which has unlabeled data. They used The Instance weighted K-Nearest Neighbor Algorithm for source domain classification; we assign each training set as learning basic and combine those models into an integrated one adaptively to give final classified value by assigning weights for each model dynamically. Knowledge is transferred from Source to target domain via Adaptive Transfer learning. Finally The Instance weighted K-Nearest Neighbor classifier trained in source domain is applied in Target domain.

# CHAPTER III
# INTER DEPENDENT DOMAIN RELEVANCE

This chapter provides the detailed description about the Inter Dependent Domain Relevance Mechanism. Inter Dependent Domain Relevance is a Feature Extraction method, the Existing System and Proposed System for feature extraction is described below.

## 3.1 DESCRIPTION OF FEATURE EXTRACTION

This section predicts the purpose of existing system with its detriments and the chore of proposed system to overcome the defects out sighted.

The vast majority of existing approaches to opinion feature extraction rely on mining patterns only from a single review corpus, ignoring the nontrivial disparities in word distributional characteristics of opinion features across different corpora. Opinions and sentiments expressed in text reviews can be generally analyzed at the document, sentence, or even phrase (word) levels

The purpose of document-level (sentence-level) opinion mining is to classify the overall subjectivity or sentiment expressed in an individual review document (sentence). for each recognized feature candidate, its domain relevance score with respect to the domain-specific and domain independent corpora is computed, which we termed the intrinsic-domain relevance (IDR) score, and the extrinsic domain relevance (EDR) score, respectively. The existing system considers only the common features present in the both reviews. The most important/ frequent features get pruned due to the unavailability of that feature in other domain. The consideration only on the common features not on the important features in domains.

## 3.2 INTER DEPENDENT DOMAIN RELEVANCE

The extraction of relevant features from the reviews is more difficult in multi domain. Whereas the Inter Dependent Domain Relevance (IDDR) mechanism is extracting the relevant and contrast domain features using domain relevance score. The features are extracted with the help of the Part-Of-Speech (POS) tagging tool. This tool generates the POS of each word in the reviews and the Noun is considered as Feature. Features (NN) are extracted based on the outcome of the tool. Based on the feature count, the Domain relevance score is generated. It is used to predict the relevance of those features in the domain.

Domain relevance score is calculates with the help of the Dispersion and Deviation. The Dispersion is calculated on basis of average weight and Standard Variance of each term present in the candidate features. Deviation is examined by average weight of each document and weight for term in the candidate features. The domain relevance score is greater than the threshold value the features are selected. The common feature is extracted and important features in that domain are also extracted.

The performance of IDDR algorithm is appropriately high compared to intrinsic domain relevance and extrinsic domain relevance algorithm. The proposed method considered two domains such as Canon S100 and iPod. The method called Inter Dependent Domain Relevance (IDDR) is predicted the features with more accuracy compare to the Intrinsic Domain Relevance

(IDR), Extrinsic Domain Relevance (EDR) and Intrinsic Extrinsic Domain Relevance (IEDR)

Efficient prediction of common features and most important features in both Canon S100 and iPod reviews.The F-Score measure indicates that the proposed method has to improve the prediction of relevant feature. This improves the efficient summarization of product reviews using the extracted features.

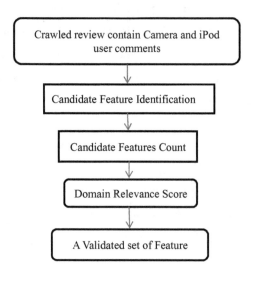

*Figure 3.1: Work Flow of Feature Extraction*

The Opinion feature extraction is shown in Figure 3.1 have following steps. Consider two different product domain such as CANON S100 domain and IPOD domain. The reviews are crawled from those product reviews. The part-of-speech (POS) of each word present in the reviews is identified with the help of the POS Tagger tool called Stanford POS tagger. The nouns are gathered from the tagger tool is considered as features. The Candidate

25

features are extracted by eliminating the repeated features. The Domain relevance score is generated with the help of the frequency count of each candidate features present in each reviews. Based on the threshold value the validated set of features is selected.

## 3.3 INTER DEPENDENT DOMAIN RELEVANCE ALGORITHM

**Algorithm 1: Validated set of opinion features**

**Input:** A domain specific/independent corpus C

**Output:** A validated list of opinion features

For each candidate feature $CF_i$ do

    For each document $D_j$ in the corpus C do

        Calculate the weight $W_{ij}$ by (3.1)

    Calculate standard variance $S_i$ by (3.3)

    Calculate dispersion $disp_i$ by (3.4)

    For each document $D_j$ in the corpus C do

        Calculate deviation $devi_{ij}$ by (3.6)

    Compute the domain relevance $dr_i$ by (3.7)

    If ($dr_i$>=threshold) then

        Confirm candidate $CF_i$ as a feature

**Return** A validated set of opinion features.

### 3.3.1 Part-Of-Speech Tagging

The reviews belonging to the product domain is send as input for Part-Of-Speech Tagger tool such as Stansford POS Tagger tool. The outcome from the tool is in the form Part-Of-Speech for each word belonging to the given reviews.The Part-Of-Speech tagging is the method of extracting the Part-Of-Speech of each word given in the input space. The features and opinions are extracted with help of the Part-Of-Speech tagging tools shown in Figure 3.2.

26

Several free tools available in online or offline to extract the features and opinion from the given reviews. Opinion words are adjectives and features are nouns.

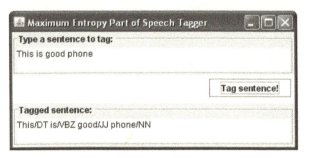

*Figure 3.2. Maximum Entropy Part of Speech Tagger*

Consider the following example. "This is good phone" – this/DT is/VBZ good/JJ book/NN

In above sentence, phone (product feature) is noun (NN) and good (opinion word) is adjective (JJ). In Part-Of-Speech tagging, each word in review is tagged with its Part-Of-Speech such as noun(NN), adverb (RB), verb(VB), conjunction (CC),pronoun (PRP) etc.After POS tagging, now it is ready to retrieve nouns as features and adjectives as opinion words. There are differently freely available POS taggers like Stanford POS tagger, Tree tagger, CRF tagger etc. Normally opinion mining use single domain to classify their thoughts. Some researcher's perform cross domain sentiment classification to improve the performance of the classification.

### 3.3.2 Candidate Features Extraction

The Features are normally in the form of Noun. So i have to extract the noun from each tagged reviews for both CANON S100 and IPOD. The repeated features are eliminated then extract the candidate features.

The sentences are crawl from the review are used to extract the features. The features are extracted based on the following rules.

Rules          Interpretation

NN+SBV->CF    Identify NN as a CF, if NN has a SBV dependency Relation

NN+VOB->CF    Identify NN as a CF, if NN has a VOB dependency Relation

NN+POB->CF    Identify NN as a CF, if NN has a POB dependency Relation

### 3.3.3 Domain relevance score (DRS)

Domain relevance score is calculates with the help of the Dispersion and Deviation. The Dispersion is calculated on basis of average weight and Standard Variance of each term present in the candidate features. Deviation is examined by average weight of each document and weight for term in the candidate features.

(i) The weight $w_{ij}$ of each Term $T_i$ in a particular document is calculated as follows.

$$w_{ij} = \begin{cases} (1 + \log TF_{ij}) \times \log\frac{N}{DF_i} & , \; if \; TF_{ij} > 0 \\ 0 & , \; Otherwise \end{cases} \text{---> (3.1)}$$

Where TF= Term Frequency, DF= Domain frequency

Where i=1...M for a total number of M terms in a document

Where j=1....N for a total number of N document in the corpus (ii)The average weight $\overline{w_i}$ of term $T_i$ is calculated as follows

$$\overline{w_i} = \frac{1}{N}\sum_{j=1}^{N} w_{ij} \text{ ---> (3.2)}$$

(iii) The Standard Variance $S_i$ for term $T_i$ is calculated as follows

$$S_i = \sqrt{\frac{\sum_{j=1}^{N}(w_{ij}-\overline{w_i})^2}{N}} \text{ ---> (3.3)}$$

(iv) The dispersion $disp_i$ of each Term $T_i$ in the Review Corpus is defined as follows.

$$disp_i = \frac{\overline{w_i}}{S_i} \text{ ---> (3.4)}$$

(v) The $\overline{w_j}$ be a average weight for a particular document across all M term as

$$\overline{w_j} = \frac{1}{M}\sum_{j=1}^{N} w_{ij} \text{ --> (3.5)}$$

(vi) The Deviation $devi_{ij}$ of the term $T_i$ in a document is expressed as follows.

$$devi_{ij} = w_{ij} - \overline{w_j} \text{ ---> (3.6)}$$

The deviation is quantified how significantly a term is used in each document in the corpus.

(vii) The Domain Relevance $dr_i$ is calculated using dispersion and deviation as follows.

$$dr_i = disp_i \times \sum_{j=1}^{N} devi_{ij} \text{ ---> (3.7)}$$

The value of $disp_i$ (for term Ti) is high, which indicate that the term frequently occur across all the document in the corpus.

DRS and Threshold value are play vital role in the selection of validated set of features. Based on the threshold value the common and most relevant features are extracted. Set 1.5 as a threshold value for IDDR algorithm.

# CHAPTER IV
# EXAGGERATE INSTANCE WEIGHTED K-NEAREST NEIGHBOR

This chapter describes the Opinion classification technique called Exaggerate Instance Weighted K-Nearest Neighbor. It includes Existing System and proposed work for the Opinion Classification.

## 4.1 GENERAL DESCRIPTION OF FEATURE OPINION SUMMARIZATION

This section predicts the purpose of existing system with its detriments and the chore of proposed system to overcome the defects out sighted.

The vast majority of existing approaches to opinion feature extraction rely on mining patterns only from a single review corpus, ignoring the nontrivial disparities in word distributional characteristics of opinion features across different corpora. Opinions and sentiments expressed in text reviews can be generally analyzed at the document, sentence, or even phrase (word) levels. The purpose of document-level (sentence-level) opinion mining is to classify the overall subjectivity or sentiment expressed in an individual review document (sentence). For each recognized feature candidate, its domain relevance score with respect to the domain-specific and domain independent corpora is computed, which we termed the intrinsic-domain relevance (IDR) score, and the extrinsic domain relevance (EDR) score, respectively. The existing system considers only the common features present in the both reviews.

For opinion classification, Likelihood ratio test is applied to the opinion word to classify the sentence into positive and negative via association rules. The semantic association is measured between the positive word and each seed word by likelihood ratio test. The classification is performed after the association rules by opinion value, upper bound and lower bound.In Transfer Learning methodology, Knowledge is transferred from Source to target domain via Adaptive Transfer learning. The Instance weighted K-Nearest Neighbor classifier trained in source domain is applied in Target domain. The neighbors are computer through the Euclidean distance.

The most important/ frequent features get pruned due to the unavailability of that feature in other domain. The consideration only on the common features not on the important features in domains.Single domain in considered and perform the likelihood ratio test.Consider similar domain but different Dataset to perform classification in EIWKNN approach.

## 4.2   EXAGGERATE   INSTANCE   WEIGHTED   K-NEAREST NEIGHBOR

In multi domain, the extraction of relevant features and Opinion classification from the reviews is more difficult. The Inter Dependent Domain Relevance (IDDR) mechanism is extracting the relevant and contrast domain features using domain relevance score. Exaggerate Instance Weighted K-Nearest Neighbor algorithm is to classify the Opinion word of two different domain via Transfer Learning.

The features and Opinion words are extracted with the help of the Part-Of-Speech (POS) tagging tool. The tool generates the POS of each word in the reviews and the Noun is considered as Feature and Adjective and Verb is

32

considered as the Opinion word. The features count in the each review is identified. Based on the feature count the Domain relevance score is generated. Domain relevance score is calculates with the help of the Dispersion and Deviation. The Dispersion is calculated on basis of average weight and Standard Variance of each term present in the candidate features. Deviation is examined by average weight of each document and weight for term in the candidate features. The domain relevance score is greater than the threshold value the features are selected.

The gathering of labeled data in every domain is not possible in every data mining process. So I move to the transfer learning to perform operation more effectively by avoiding much expensive data.The Exaggerate Instance Weighted K-Nearest Neighbor algorithm performs the classification with great accurate classifier. Cross validation is the process to improve and identify the accuracy of the classifier. The accuracy of the classifier can be increased during each round of the cross validation until it reach the maximum accuracy. Normally the opinion classification only considers the opinion word. Sometimes the polarity (Opinion) of the opinion word can change due to the prior polarity word. EIWKNN approaches consider the prior polarity before it finalizes the polarity of the opinion word.

The summarization is the final step of the feature based opinion summarization. The summarization is in the form of each feature with their corresponding strongly positive, weakly positive, neutral, strongly negative and weakly negative opinion sentence.The proposed method considered two domains such as Canon S100 and iPod. The performance of IDDR algorithm is appropriately high compared to intrinsic domain relevance and extrinsic domain relevance algorithm. The comparative analysis proves that the

EIWKNN algorithm is more effective than the Support Vector Machine and K-Nearest Neighbor.

Efficient prediction of common features and most important features in both Canon S100 and iPod reviews.The knowledge transfer leads to reduce the cost of collecting the labeled data of each domain. Prior polarity concept is highly improves the opinion classification.The F-Score measure indicates that the proposed method has to improve the prediction capacity. This improves the efficient summarization of product reviews.

## 4.3 SYSTEM ARCHITECTURE

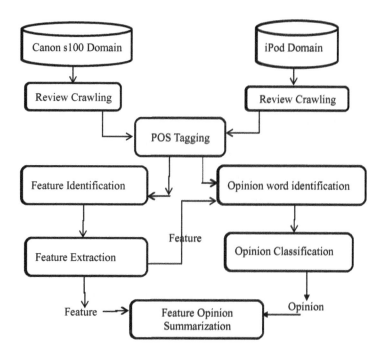

*Figure 4.1. System Architecture*

The System Architecture of the Feature based Opinion Summarization is shown in Figure 4.1. Initially the Reviews are crawled from the two different domain corpuses. Use part-of-speech Tagging, the Features and Opinion words are identified. The collected features are grouped to form feature list. The valid set of features is extracted from the features list using Inter Dependent Domain Relevance mechanism. The Valid set of Features is used to identify the relevant sentence from the domain corpus. The opinion words are identified using POS tagging. The Identifier is generates the score from the online sentiment prediction tool. The identified opinion word is sent to the identifier from where the opinion is predicted. The Exaggerate Instance Weighted K-Nearest Neighbor algorithm classifies the opinion word into strongly positive, weakly positive, strongly negative, weakly negative and neutral. Based on the features and predicted opinion the summary has been generated.

## 4.4 OPINION CLASSIFICATION

The classification for two different domains has been performed. Initially the user comments are gathered from the web contains two different domains such as camera and iPod. The labeled review sentences of camera domain are separated as training domain and unlabeled review sentences of camera and iPod are considered as test domain.

The cross validation of training dataset has been performed by EIWKNN algorithm through assigning of weight to each sentence present in the training dataset. Based on the KNN algorithm, learning rate, error, accuracy the reassignment of weight has been performed. The highly accurate classifier is now ready to perform classification. The unlabeled sentences are sent to the EIWKNN algorithm. Each unlabeled sentences in the test domain is finding nearest neighbor through mapping sentence concept and k value. The class of the unlabeled sentence is assign by the sum of weight and class of each neighbor. Finally the summarization of the positive, negative and mixed sentence is formed. The Opinion Prediction is carried out in two different domains using EIWKNN algorithm is explained below, the steps are shown in Figure 4.2.

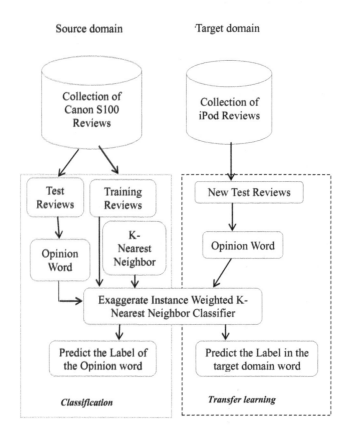

Figure 4.2: Opinion Prediction

**Algorithm 1: Classification using K-Nearest Neighbor**

**Input:** Labeled Reviews $D_{tr}$ and Unlabeled Review $D_{te}$

**Output:** Labeled Review u

**Initialization:**

(i) $D_n$=empty

For each unlabeled Opinion word u in $D_{te}$

For each Labeled Opinion word l in $D_{tr}$

If $|N|<K$

Then $D_n = D_n \cup u$

Else

If $n \in D_n$ such that dist(l,u)$\geq$ dist(l,n)

Then

$D_n=D_n-n$

$D_n=D_n \cup l$

Return $M_C$ by (6)


**Algorithm 2: Cross-Validation using Exaggerate Instance Weighted K-Nearest Neighbor**

**Input:** Labeled Reviews Dl

**Output:** Optimized Labeled Review Dl

**Initialization:**

(i) Assign K =5

(ii) Randomly assign Weight for all sentences in Dtr

(iii) Dn=null

Step1: Split the $D_{tr}$ into two parts $D_{t1}$, $D_{t2}$

Step 1.1: Set $D_{t1}$ as train and $D_{t2}$ as test do step 2

Step 1.2: Set $D_{t1}$ as test and $D_{t2}$ as train do step 2

Step2:    set train as $D_{tr}$ and Test as $D_{te}$ goto alg 1

Step 3: for each te in $D_{te}$ do

If($O_{Ci}$!=$M_{Ci}$)

Find Error by (8)

Reassign weight by (7)

Step 4: Find Accuracy by (9)

Step 5: if($Acc_{n-1}$<_$Acc_n$)

Goto step 2

Else

Return

### 4.4.1 Feature Opinion Summarization

Consider two different product domain such as CANON S100 domain and IPOD domain. The reviews are crawled from those product reviews. The part-of-speech (POS) of each word present in the reviews is identified with the help of the POS Tagger tool called Stanford POS tagger. The nouns are gathered from the tagger tool is considered as features. The Candidate features are extracted by eliminating the repeated features. The Domain relevance score is generated with the help of the frequency count of each candidate features present in each reviews. Based on the threshold value the validated set of features is selected.

The cross validation of the $D_{tr}$ is performed by the instance weighted K nearest neighbor algorithm. Here two folds are formed. One fold is considered as train and another one is considered as test. The first loop run consider first half as train second half as est. the second loop is run by considered second half as train and first half as test dataset.

38

The weight of the each tuples or sentences, k value and temporary variable are initialized before starting the cross validation. The temporary storage has the capacity of k number of word. Consider each opinion word of test sentence and finding their closest neighbor from training sentence using hamming distance. Consider an example, word1 is Charm and word2 is Chafe. The hamming Distance between Charm and Chafe is 2.

Initially find k closest neighbor from training sentences and check their hamming distance of newly added training opinion word. If the newly added word has minimum distance compared to previously added opinion word means add the new word and eliminate the old word. Continuous their process until it reach last opinion word in the training tuple. The k number of neighbor is now ready to predict the class value by (4.1)

$$M_C = \Sigma_K W_k C_k \rightarrow (4.1)$$

The above process can performed in all test instances. Then reassign the weight of wrongly predicted instance using old weight, learning rate (assume 0.2) and error by (4.2).

$$W_{rk} = W_{ak} + (\alpha * Err) \rightarrow (4.2)$$

$$Err_i = O_{ci} - M_{ci} \rightarrow (4.3)$$

The accuracy of the classifier is predicted by (4.4). The cross validation is again performed when the newly predicted accuracy is higher than the previously predicted accuracy.

$$Acc_n = \left(\frac{Correctly\ modified\ instances}{Total\ instances}\right) * 100 \rightarrow (4.4)$$

The highly accurate classifier is formed for the prediction of unlabeled data in source and target domain. Consider each word present in unlabeled sentences and perform the EIWKNN algorithm for each opinion word find the k number of closest neighbor using Hamming distance. The temporary storage is used to store the k number of neighbor. The temporary storage is first filled by first k number of neighbor then the next tuple is added when the distance of new tuple is minimum compared to the previously added opinion word. Finally the class can be predicted by using (6). The prior polarity of the opinion word is considered after found the opinion through KNN. If the opinion word has negative prior polarity means reverse the opinion, otherwise return the predicted opinion.

The summarization is the final step of the feature based opinion summarization. The summarization is in the form of each feature with their corresponding strongly positive, weakly positive, strongly negative, weakly negative and neutral opinion sentence.

**Example 1:**

Feature: "Memory"

STRONGLY POSITIVE:

Sentence 1: The Memory capacity is Excellent

Sentence 2: I admire the Memory size

...

WEAKLY POSITIVE:

Sentence 1: The Memory of the Canon S100 is not bad.

Sentence 2: Canon S100's memory is fair

...

WEAKLY NEGATIVE:

Sentence 1: Need improvement in memory size

Sentence 2: Memory size is not enough

...

STRONGLY NEGATIVE:

Sentence 1: Memory size is too low.

Sentence 2: Its Memory capacity is very poor.

...

# CHAPTER V

# RESULTS AND DISCUSSION

This section describes the performance analysis to validate the proposed algorithm. The domain such as Canon S100 (camera), iPod are used for the predicting the Opinion accuracy in Support Vector Machine (SVM), K-Nearest Neighbor (KNN) and Exaggerate Instance Weighted K-Nearest Neighbor (EIWKNN).

## 5.1 SOFTWARE DESCRIPTION

### 5.1.1 Introduction to JAVA

Java is a programming language originally developed by James Gosling at Sun Microsystems (now a subsidiary of Oracle Corporation) and released in 1995 as a core component of Sun Microsystems' Java platform. The language derives much of its syntax from C and C++ but has a simpler object model and fewer low-level facilities. Java applications are typically compiled to byte code (class file) that can run on any Java Virtual Machine (JVM) regardless of computer architecture.

Java is a general-purpose, concurrent, class-based, object-oriented language that is specifically designed to have as few implementation dependencies as possible. It is intended to let application developers "write once, run anywhere." Java is currently one of the most popular programming languages in use, particularly for client-server web applications.

### 5.1.2. JAVA Platform

One characteristic of Java is portability, which means that computer programs written in the Java language must run similarly on any hardware/operating-system platform. This is achieved by compiling the Java language code to an intermediate representation called Java byte code, instead of directly to platform-specific machine code. Java byte code instructions are analogous to machine code, but are intended to be interpreted by a virtual machine (VM) written specifically for the host hardware. End-users commonly use a Java Runtime Environment (JRE) installed on their own machine for standalone Java applications, or in a Web browser for Java applets. Standardized libraries provide a generic way to access host-specific features such as graphics, threading, and networking. A major benefit of using byte code is porting. However, the overhead of interpretation means that interpreted programs almost always run more slowly than programs compiled to native executable would.

Just-in-Time compilers were introduced from an early stage that compiles byte codes to machine code during runtime. Just as application servers such as Glassfish provide lifecycle services to web applications, the Net Beans runtime container provides them to Swing applications. Application servers understand how to compose web modules, EJB modules, and so on, into a single web application, just as the Net Beans runtime container understands how to compose Net Beans modules into a single Swing application. Modularity offers a solution to "JAR hell" by letting developers organize their code into strictly separated and versioned modules. Only those that have explicitly declared dependencies on each other are able to use code from each other's exposed packages.

"Projects/org-netbeans-modules-java-j2seproject/Lookup"      folder's content is used to construct the project's additional lookup. Its content is expected to be Lookup Provider instances. J2SE project provides Lookup Mergers for Sources, Privileged Templates and Recommended Templates. Implementations added by 3rd parties will be merged into a single instance in the project's lookup. The keyword static in front of a method indicates a static method, which is associated only with the class and not with any specific instance of that class. Only static methods can be invoked without a reference to an object. Static methods cannot access any class members that are not also static.

The method name "main" is not a keyword in the Java language. It is simply the name of the method the Java launcher calls to pass control to the program. The main method must accept an array of String objects. By convention, it is referenced as args although any other legal identifier name can be used. Since Java 5, the main method can also use variable arguments, in the form of public static void main (String... args), allowing the main method to be invoked with an arbitrary number of String arguments.

### 5.1.3 APPLET BASICS

The Applet class is contained in the java.applet package. Applet contains several methods that give you detailed control over the execution of your applet. In addition, java.applet also defines three interfaces: AppletContext, AudioClip, and AppletStub.All applets are subclasses of Applet. Thus, all applets must import java.applet. Applets must also import java.awt. Recall that AWT stands for the Abstract Window Toolkit. Since all applets run in a window, it is necessary to include support for that window. Applets are not executed by the console-based Java run-time interpreter.

Rather, they are executed by either a Web browser or an applet viewer. We have to create with the standard applet viewer, called appletviewer, provided by the JDK. But it can use any applet viewer or browser.

Execution of an applet does not begin at main( ). Actually, few applets even have main( ) methods. Instead, execution of an applet is started and controlled with an entirely different mechanism, which will be explained shortly. Output to the applet's window is not performed by System.out.println( ). Rather, it is handled with various AWT methods,such as drawString( ), which outputs a string to a specified X,Y location. Input is also handled differently than in an application.

Once an applet has been compiled, it is included in an HTML file using the APPLET tag. The applet will be executed by a Java-enabled web browser when it encounters the APPLET tag within the HTML file. To view and test an applet more conveniently, simply include a comment at the head of the Java source code file that contains the APPLET tag. This way, the code is documented with the necessary HTML statements needed by the applet, and we can test the compiled applet by starting the applet viewer with your Java source code file specified as the target.

### 5.1.4 Abstract Window Toolkit

The Abstract Window Toolkit (AWT) was introduced because it provides support for applets. The AWT contains numerous classes and methods that allow you to create and manage windows. To create and manage windows, manage fonts, output text, and utilize graphics. It contains the various controls, such as scroll bars and push buttons, supported by the AWT. It also explains further aspects of Java's event handling mechanism and examines the AWT's imaging subsystem and animation. Although the main purpose of the AWT is to support applet windows, it can also be used to create stand-alone windows that run in a GUI environment, such as Windows.

## 5.2 EXPERIMENTAL RESULTS

This section describes the performance analysis to validate the EIWKNN algorithm.

### 5.2.1 F-SCORE

The performances are measured using the standard evaluation measures of precision ($p$), recall ($r$) and F-score ($F$), $F = 2pr/(p+r)$. They are able to improve the recall dramatically without much loss in precision. The gains in F-scores are dramatic. Naturally as the number of given opinion words increases, the improvement decreases slightly.

$$F - Score = \frac{Recall \times Precision}{\frac{(Recall+Precision)}{2}} \longrightarrow (5.1)$$

| Alg/Review | c1 | c2 | c3 | c4 | c5 | c6 |
|---|---|---|---|---|---|---|
| SVM | 0.680222 | 0.511712 | 0.732245 | 0.579832 | 0.74972 | 0.654373 |
| KNN | 0.610351 | 0.558318 | 0.626118 | 0.28943 | 0.582638 | 0.616551 |
| EIWKNN | 0.872759 | 0.885294 | 0.877974 | 0.8 | 0.878253 | 0.848385 |

Table 5.1 F-Score

46

The F-Score value of Figure 5.1 is calculated based on the precision and Recall value. The precision and recall proves that the EIWKNN is more efficient this lead to the F-Score also shows that the EIWKNN is more efficient than other three algorithms. The predication capacity of EIWKNN is 60% more than the other two approaches.

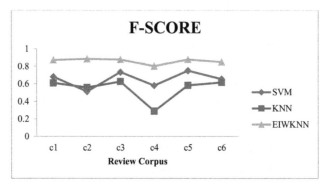

*Figure 5.1: F-SCORE*

## 5.2.2 PRECISION

In information retrieval, precision is the fraction of retrieved documents that are relevant to search. Similarly, in opinion word or feature exaction algorithm precision is the fraction of retrieved opinion words/ features that are relevant to search.

$$Precision = \frac{|\{relevant\ opinion\ features\} \cap \{retrieved\ opinion\ features\}|}{|\{retrieved\ opinion\ features\}|} \rightarrow (5.2)$$

| Alg/Review | c1 | c2 | c3 | c4 | c5 | c6 |
|---|---|---|---|---|---|---|
| SVM | 0.6714 | 0.71 | 0.69 | 0.5 | 0.782 | 0.787 |
| KNN | 0.655 | 0.611 | 0.699 | 0.294 | 0.698 | 0.571 |
| EIWKNN | 0.889 | 0.872 | 0.9 | 0.8 | 0.935 | 0.903 |

*Table 5.2 Precision*

In Figure 5.2, the IDDR curve lies well above the IDR, EDR and IEDR curve for all. This is perfectly acceptable since Precision values at high levels are more practical. Across all Precision levels, the largest gap of IDDR over IDR is 0.3. The Proposed IEDR thus achieved a significant improvement over IDR, EDR and IEDR.

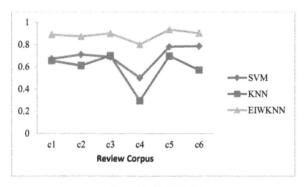

*Figure 5.2: PRECISION*

## 5.2.3 RECALL

In information retrieval, recall is the fraction of the documents that are relevant to the query that are successfully retrieved. In opinion word extraction or feature exaction algorithm, recall will be the fraction of the relevant opinion words or features that are relevant to that are successfully retrieved.

48

$$Recall = \frac{|\{relevant\ opinion\ features\} \cap \{retrieved\ opinion\ features\}|}{|\{relevant\ opinion\ wfeatures\}|} \rightarrow (5.3)$$

| Alg/Review | c1 | c2 | c3 | c4 | c5 | c6 |
|---|---|---|---|---|---|---|
| SVM | 0.6901 | 0.4 | 0.78 | 0.69 | 0.72 | 0.56 |
| KNN | 0.5714 | 0.514 | 0.567 | 0.285 | 0.5 | 0.67 |
| EIWKNN | 0.8571 | 0.899 | 0.857 | 0.8 | 0.828 | 0.8 |

*Table 5.3 Recall*

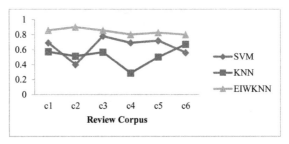

*Figure 5.3: Recall*

In Figure 5.3, the IDDR curve lies well above the IDR, EDR and IEDR curve for all. This is perfectly acceptable since Recall values at high levels are more practical. Across all Recall levels, the largest gap of IDDR over IDR is 0.3 in r3. The Proposed IEDR thus achieved a significant improvement over IDR, EDR and IEDR.

# CHAPTER VI

# CONCLUSION AND FUTURE ENHANCEMENT

The Feature based opinion summarization was carried out with Inter Dependent Domain Relevance and Exaggerate Instance Weighted K-Nearest Neighbor algorithm with the great accuracy. IDDR is the opinion feature extraction based on the Domain Relevance Score which utilizes the disparities in distributional characteristics of features across two corpora, one domain-specific (canon S100) and one domain-independent (iPod). IDDR identifies candidate features that are specific to the given review domain and also specifies the most important features in the both domain. Experimental results demonstrate that the proposed IDDR not only leads to noticeable improvement over either Intrinsic Domain Relevance (IDR) or Extrinsic Domain Relevance (EDR), but also outperforms on Intrinsic Extrinsic Domain Relevance feature extraction results. Both IDR and EDR are in-domain feature extraction mechanism and IEDR is cross-domain feature extraction. The extraction of features is not only the common features but also the most important features in each domain. In addition, since a good quality domain-independent corpus is quite important for the proposed approach. The Opinion Classification is done using Exaggerate Instance Weighted K-Nearest Neighbor algorithm. The knowledge from camera domain to iPod domain is transferred using labeled camera data and EIWKNN algorithm. The Cross validation improves the accuracy of the classifier. The labels such as Positive, Negative and neutral are classified with the weight and class of the K number of Neighbors. The comparative analysis proves that the EIWKNN algorithm is more effective than the Support Vector Machine and K-Nearest Neighbor.

For future work, (1) Consider more than two domains and perform IDDR feature extraction mechanism with improved accuracy. (2) To jointly identify opinion features, including non-noun features, infrequent features, as well as implicit features. (3) Classify the product reviews as positive, negative and neutral polarity as well as weakly positive, mildly positive, strongly positive, weakly negative, mildly negative and strongly negative using the extracted validated set of features. (4) I plan to further test the IDDR opinion feature extraction in several other opinion mining systems. (5) Summarization of features with respect to their opinion word is performed.

# APPENDEX 1

## SOURCE CODE

**Read the review**

```java
import java.io.*;
import java.util.Scanner;
import java.sql.*;
class read
{
ResultSet rs=null,rs1=null;
Connection con=null;
Statement stmt=null;
read()
{
try
        {
        Class.forName("sun.jdbc.odbc.JdbcOdbcDriver");
        con=DriverManager.getConnection("jdbc:odbc:nokia");
        stmt=con.createStatement(ResultSet.TYPE_SCROLL_SENSITIVE,Re
sultSet.CONCUR_UPDATABLE);
try
{
rs.close();
}
catch(Exception ee){}
String aa="",ab="";
        File file=new File("C:/Users/acer/Desktop/abirami/nokia 6600
review/nokia review4 tagged.txt");
                try
                {
                Scanner input=new Scanner(file);
                while(input.hasNext())
```

```
                {
                        String word1=input.next();//System.out.println("a");
                        if(word1.contains("_NN"))
                        {
aa=word1;
String se[]=aa.split("_");
stmt.executeUpdate("insert into n4fea values('"+se[0]+"')");
                        }
                }}
catch(Exception err){}
}
catch(Exception tt){}
}}
```

**Domain Relevance Score**

```
public class mdr extends JFrame
{
JLabel l4=new JLabel("Features");
JLabel l1=new JLabel("Score");
JLabel l2=new JLabel("Validation");
TextArea a1,a2,a3,a4,a5;
ResultSet rs1=null,rs2=null;
Connection con=null;
Statement stmt=null;
String a[]=new String[500];
String nn;
int aa[]=new int[500];
int i=0;
mdr()
{
super("DOMAIN RELEVANCE SCORE");
setLayout(null);
 l4.setBounds(30,5,100,20);add(l4);
l1.setBounds(210,5,100,20);add(l1);
l2.setBounds(300,5,150,20);add(l2);
a1=new TextArea(15,20);
a1.setBounds(20,40,400,350);
add(l1);
```

```java
add(a1);
dbopen1();
}
public void dbopen1()
{
try
{
Class.forName("sun.jdbc.odbc.JdbcOdbcDriver");
con=DriverManager.getConnection("jdbc:odbc:multi");
stmt=con.createStatement(ResultSet.TYPE_SCROLL_SENSITIVE,ResultSet
.CONCUR_UPDATABLE);
rs1=stmt.executeQuery("Select * from ssheet1");
while(rs1.next())
{
a[i]=rs1.getString("feat");
nn=a[i];
aa[i]=nn.length();
i++;
}
i=0; rs1.close();
rs2=stmt.executeQuery("Select * from ssheet1");
while(rs2.next())
{
a1.append(a[i]);
if(aa[i]==8)
a1.append("\t        \t");
else if(aa[i]>7)
a1.append("\t          \t");
else
a1.append("\t    \t   \t");
String xx,xy;
xx=rs2.getString("dr");
a1.append(xx);
if(xx.contains("E"))
a1.append("\t\t\t"); else
a1.append("\t");
xx=rs2.getString("prune");
```

```
a1.append(xx);a1.append("\t");
a1.append("\n");
i++;
} }
catch(Exception e1) {}
}public void dbclose()
{
try
{
stmt.close();rs1.close();rs2.close();con.close();
}
catch(NullPointerException ie) { }
catch(SQLException i) { }
}
```

# APPENDIX 2

# SNAPSHOTS

## A 2.1. Two Different Domain Feature Summarization

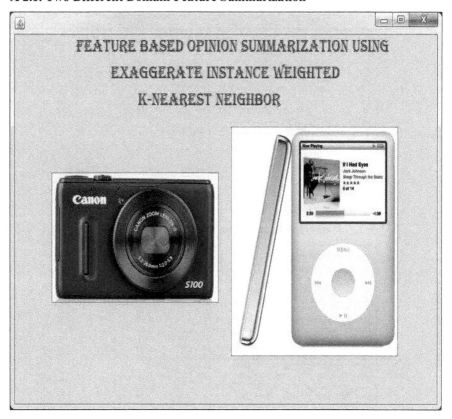

## A 2.2. Camera Domain

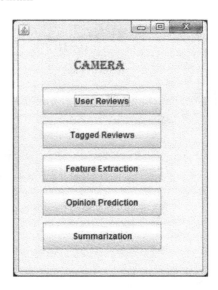

## A 2.3. Camera Domain User Reviews

## A 2.4. Tagged Camera User Reviews

## A 2.5. Feature Extraction

## A 2.6. Feature List and Pruned Features

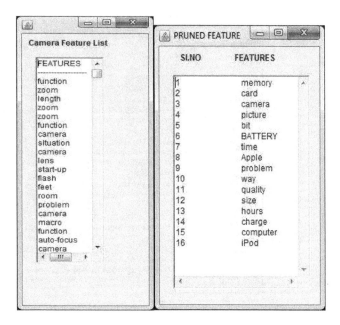

## A 2.7. Opinion Prediction

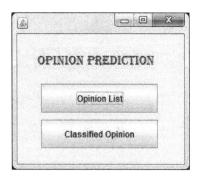

## A 2.8. Opinion Word List and Classified Opinion Word

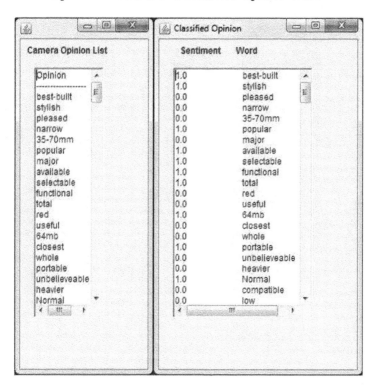

## A 2.9. Selection of Features

60

## A 2.10. Summarization of Camera Reviews

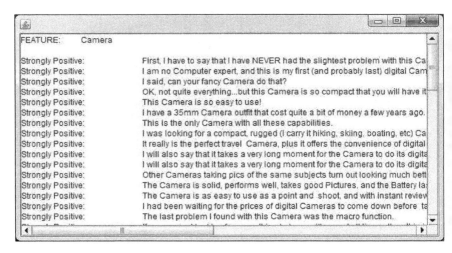

## A 2.11. Selection of Features

## A 2.12 Summarization of Reviews

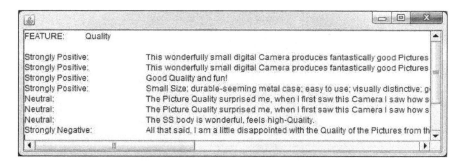

## A 2.13. iPod Domain

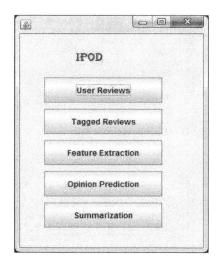

## A 2.14. iPod Domain User Reviews

iPod reviews

The iPod has so far been one of the most advertised and
players so far. I'm still figuring out why. There isn't much fi
iPod at all, except games. My friend has this unit while no
much, I look at other reviews on this site and tried out the
at Best Buy, and it's definitely the most overrated gadget in
sound quality is pretty good. The Creative player sounds a
anything to worry about. It has an equalizer, but the iRiver
lot more presets than the iPod. The bass is deep and the
clear. Not good. First problem, if you haven't seen the new
are being recalled for battery problems and not lasting the
is really stupid to me. 18 months for a battery isn't good, a
mediocre. iRiver's battery lasts four to five years. Also, the
However, the Creative and iRiver players are (Rio's isn't),
$30 to replace, while iPod charges shipping and technica
years. Another thing you should know, the metal on the flip
iPod is very tacky, and scratches very easily. While all MP:
to scratch, the iPod is the worst of the Creative and iRiver.
liking the gel case. iRiver's seems a lot more sturdier tha
there aren't any features, unless you call the games a fea
FM tuner, while there is no FM tuner on the Creative Zen (
micro version of the Zen there is a tuner), the iRiver H10-2
Karma, and the iAudio X5 have FM tuners. There is also n
something most if not all MP3 players have that the iPod i

## A 2.15. Tagged iPod User Reviews

iPod Tagged reviews

The_DT iPod_NNP has_VBZ so_RB far_RB been_VBN o
players_NNS so_RB far_RB ._. I_PRP 'm_VBP still_RB fi
much_JJ features_NNS on_IN the_DT iPod_NN at_IN all
this_DT unit_NN while_IN not_RB experience_VB it_PRP
this_DT site_NN and_CC tried_VBD out_RP the_DT unit
definitely_RB the_DT most_RBS overrated_JJ gadget_N
pretty_RB good_JJ ._. The_DT Creative_JJ player_NN so
to_TO worry_VB about_RB ._. It_PRP has_VBZ an_DT eq
a_DT lot_NN more_JJR presets_NNS than_IN the_DT iP
treble_NN is_VBZ clear_JJ ._. Not_RB good_JJ ._. First_.
seen_VBN the_DT news_NN recently_RB ._. the_DT iPo
not_RB lasting_VBG the_DT advertised_VBN 18_CD mo
18_CD months_NNS for_IN a_DT battery_NN is_VBZ n't
._. iRiver_NNP 's_POS battery_NN lasts_VBZ four_CD to
's_POS ARE_VBP N'T_RB USER_NNP REPLACEABLE_
-LRB-_-LRB- Rio_NNP 's_POS is_VBZ n't_RB -RRB-_-R
to_TO replace_VB ._. while_IN iPod_NN charges_NNS s
battery_NN ._. 1.5_CD years_NNS ._. Another_DT thing_
the_DT flip_JJ side_NN of_IN the_DT iPod_NN is_VBZ ve
._. While_IN all_DT MP3_NN players_NNS are_VBP eas
worst_JJS of_IN the_DT Creative_JJ and_CC iRiver_NNF
There_EX is_VBZ no_DT photo_NN viewing_NN option_
photo_NN iPod_NN __ but_CC it_PRP costs_VBZ $_$ 2

63

## A 2.16. Feature Extraction

## A 2.17. iPod Features List and Pruned Features

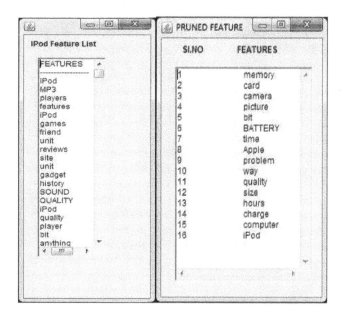

## A 2.18. Opinion Prediction

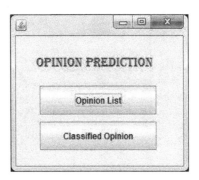

## A 2.19. iPod Opinion Word List and Classified Opinion

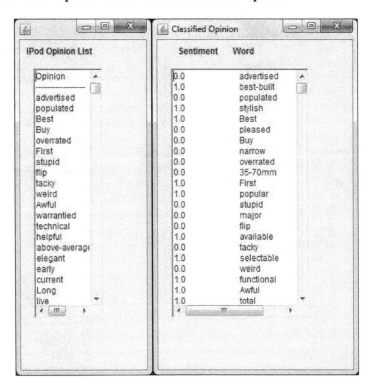

## A 2.20. Selecting Feature for Summarization

## A 2.21. Summarization of User Reviews

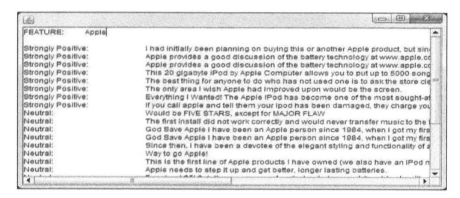

## A 2.22. Selecting Feature for Summarization

## A 2.23. Summarization of User Reviews

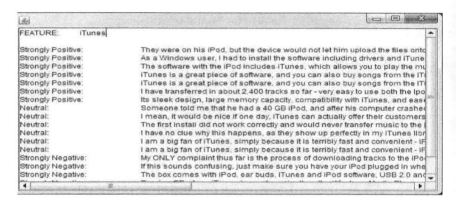

FEATURE:        iTunes

| | |
|---|---|
| Strongly Positive: | They were on his iPod, but the device would not let him upload the files ontc |
| Strongly Positive: | As a Windows user, I had to install the software including drivers and iTune |
| Strongly Positive: | The software with the iPod includes iTunes, which allows you to play the mu |
| Strongly Positive: | iTunes is a great piece of software, and you can also buy songs from the iT |
| Strongly Positive: | iTunes is a great piece of software, and you can also buy songs from the iT |
| Strongly Positive: | I have transferred in about 2,400 tracks so far - very easy to use both the ipo |
| Strongly Positive: | Its sleek design, large memory capacity, compatibility with iTunes, and ease |
| Neutral: | Someone told me that he had a 40 GB iPod, and after his computer crashec |
| Neutral: | I mean, it would be nice if one day, iTunes can actually offer their customers |
| Neutral: | The first install did not work correctly and would never transfer music to the I |
| Neutral: | I have no clue why this happens, as they show up perfectly in my iTunes libr |
| Neutral: | I am a big fan of iTunes, simply because it is terribly fast and convenient - IF |
| Neutral: | I am a big fan of iTunes, simply because it is terribly fast and convenient - IF |
| Strongly Negative: | My ONLY complaint thus far is the process of downloading tracks to the iPo |
| Strongly Negative: | If this sounds confusing, just make sure you have your iPod plugged in whe |
| Strongly Negative: | The box comes with iPod, ear buds, iTunes and iPod software, USB 2.0 and |

# REFERENCES

1. Bing Liu. (2011), "Sentiment Analysis Tutorial" – Given at AAAI-2011, San Francisco, USA.

2. Blei D.M. Ng A.Y. and Jordan M.I. (2003), "Latent Dirichlet Allocation," J. Machine Learning Research, vol. 3, pp. 993-1022.

3. Bollegala D. Weir D. and Carroll J. (2013), "Cross-Domain Sentiment Classification Using a Sentiment Sensitive Thesaurus," IEEE Trans. Knowledge and Data Eng., vol. 25, no. 8, pp. 1719-1731.

4. Cai D. He X. Han J. and Huang T. S. (2011), "Graph regularized nonnegative matrix factorization for data representation," IEEE Transactions on Pattern Analysis and Machine Intelligence, vol. 33, no. 8, pp. 1548–1560.

5. Dave K. Lawrence S. and Pennock D. (2003), "Mining the peanut gallery: opinion extraction and semantic classification of product reviews." WWW'.

6. Ding C. Li T. and Peng W. (2006), "Nonnegative matrix factorization and probabilistic latent semantic indexing: Equivalence, chisquare statistic, and a hybrid method," in Proceedings of the 21st AAAI Conference on Artificial Intelligence, ser. AAAI.

7. Dunning T. (1993), "Accurate Methods for the Statistics of Surprise and Coincidence," Computational Linguistics, vol. 19, no. 1, pp. 61-74.

8. Esuli A.and Fabrizio Sebastiani. (2006), SENTIWORDNET: A Publicly Available Lexical Resource for Opinion Mining. In Proceedings of LREC.

9. Hai Z. Chang K. Song Q. and J. Kim J. (2010), "A Statistical Nlp Approach for Feature and Sentiment Identification from Chinese Reviews," Proc. CIPS-SIGHAN Joint Conf. Chinese Language Processing, pp. 105-112.

10. John Blitzer. (2007)"Domain Adaptation of Natural Language Processing Systems," PhD thesis, The University of Pennsylvania.

11. Jin W. and Ho H.H. (2009), "A Novel Lexicalized HMM-Based Learning Framework for Web Opinion Mining," Proc. 26th Ann. Int'l Conf. Machine Learning, pp. 465-472.

12. Kim S.M. and Hovy E. (2006), "Extracting Opinions, Opinion Holders, and Topics Expressed in Online News Media Text," Proc. ACL/COLING Workshop Sentiment and Subjectivity in Text.

13. Li F. Han C. Huang M., Zhu X. Y. Xia J. Zhang S. and Yu H. (2010), "Structure-Aware Review Mining and Summarization," Proc. 23$^{rd}$Int'l Conf. Computational Linguistics, pp. 653-661.

14. Liu B. (2012), "Sentiment Analysis and Opinion Mining," Synthesis Lectures on Human Language Technologies, vol. 5, no. 1, pp. 1-167.

15. Maas A.L. Daly R.E. Pham P.T. Huang D. Ng A.Y. and Potts C. (2011), "Learning Word Vectors for Sentiment Analysis," Proc. 49th Ann. Meeting of the Assoc. for Computational Linguistics: Human Language Technologies, pp. 142-150.

16. Pang B. Lee L. and Vaithyanathan S. (2002), "Thumbs up?: Sentiment Classification Using Machine Learning Techniques," Proc. Conf. Empirical Methods in Natural Language Processing, pp. 79-86.

17. Pang B. and Lee, L. (2004). "A sentimental education: sentiment analysis using subjectivity summarization based on minimum cuts." In Proceedings of the 42nd Annual Meeting on Association for Computational Linguistics (Barcelona, Spain, July 21 - 26, 2004).

18. Pan S.J. and Yang Q. (2010), "A Survey on Transfer Learning," IEEE Trans. Knowledge and Data Eng., vol. 22, no. 10, pp. 1345-1359.

19. Popescu A. and Etzioni O. (2005), "Extracting Product Features and Opinions from Reviews," Proc. Human Language Technology Conf.and Conf. Empirical Methods in Natural Language Processing, pp. 339-346.

20. Qu L. Ifrim G. and Weikum G. (2010), "The Bag-of-Opinions Method for Review Rating Prediction from Sparse Text Patterns," Proc. 23rd Int'l Conf. Computational Linguistics, pp. 913-921.

21. Qiu G. Liu B. Bu J. and Chen C. (2011), "Opinion Word Expansion and Target Extraction through Double Propagation," Computational Linguistics, vol. 37, pp. 9-27.

22. Qiu G. Wang C. Bu J. Liu K. and Chen C. (2008), "Incorporate the Syntactic Knowledge in Opinion Mining in User-Generated Content," Proc. WWW 2008 Workshop NLP Challenges in he Information Explosion Era.

23. Sanju P. Abirami R. Sheelarani N. (2013), "Wind Turbine Power Classification using Adaptive Transfer Learning," Proc. National Conference on architecture, software systems and green computing.

24. Tong, R.M. (2001) "An operational system for detecting and tracking opinions in on-line discussions," Working Notes of the ACM SIGIR 2001 Workshop on Operational Text Classification (pp. 1-6). New York, NY: ACM.

25. Turney P.D. (2002), "Thumbs Up or Thumbs Down?: Semantic Orientation Applied to Unsupervised Classification of Reviews," Proc. 40th Ann. Meeting on Assoc. for Computational Linguistics, pp. 417-424.

26. Whitelaw, C., Garg, N., and Argamon, S. (2005), "Using appraisal groups for sentiment analysis." In Proceedings of the 14th ACM international Conference on information and Knowledge Management (Bremen, Germany, October 31 - November 05, 2005). CIKM '05. ACM, New York, NY, 625- 631.

27. Wilson T. Wiebe J. and Hoffmann P. (2005), "Recognizing Contextual Polarity in Phrase-Level Sentiment Analysis," Proc. Conf. Human Language Technology and Empirical Methods in Natural Language Processing, pp. 347-354.

28. Zhen Hai, Kuiyu Chang, Jung-Jae Kim, and Christopher C. Yang (2014), "Identifying Features in Opinion Mining via Intrinsic and Extrinsic Domain Relevance," ieee transactions on knowledge and data engineering, vol. 26, no. 3.

29. Zhu X. and Lafferty J. (2005), "Harmonic mixtures: combining mixture models and graph-based methods for inductive and scalable semi-supervised learning," in Proceedings of the 22$^{nd}$ International Conference on Machine Learning, ser. ICML.

30. Zhuang L. Feng Jing and Xiaoyan Zhu. (2006) "Movie Review Mining and Summarization." In Proceedings of CIKM.